A Nation Starts with Great People

CONTENTS

A Visit to Mount Vernon	page 4
Immigrants Stopped Here	page 18

NATIONAL GEOGRAPHIC School Publishing
Hampton-Brown

Words with Schwa

Look at the pictures. Read the words.
The dark letters all sound the same!

Example:

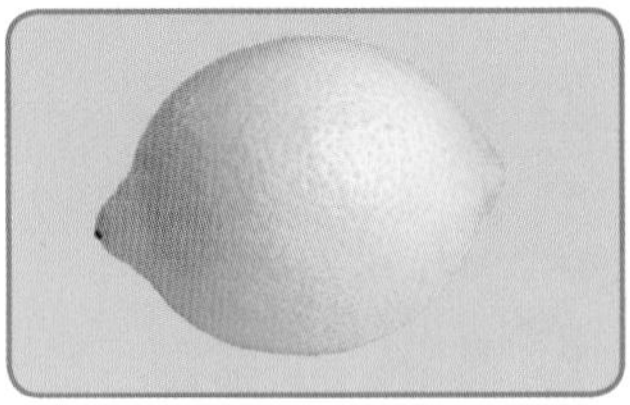

lem**o**n

muff**i**n

gard**e**n

cam**e**l

med**a**l

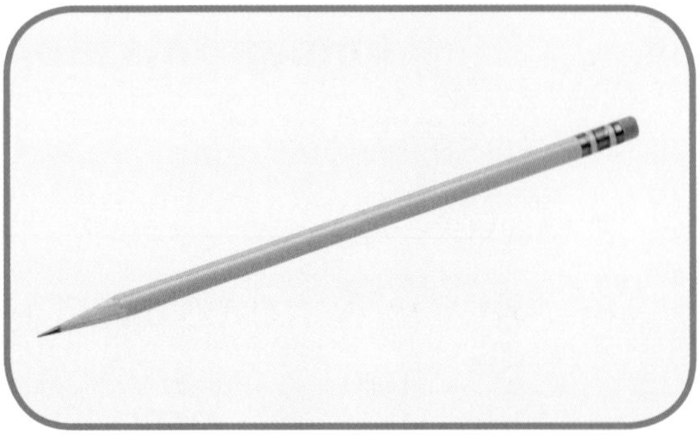

penc**i**l

High Frequency
Words

- ate
- bed
- big
- came
- floor
- home
- left
- life
- new
- sure

Key Words

Look at the pictures. Read the sentences.

What do you think the visitors ate for dinner?

A Big Home

1. This **big home** is old, not **new**.
2. The **bed** and **floor** are old, too.
3. People had a good **life** in that home.
4. Many visitors **came**. They were **sure** they would have a good time.
5. Some of these visitors **left** after they **ate** dinner.

Phonics Games
NGReach.com

A Visit to Mount Vernon

by Karen Cotton

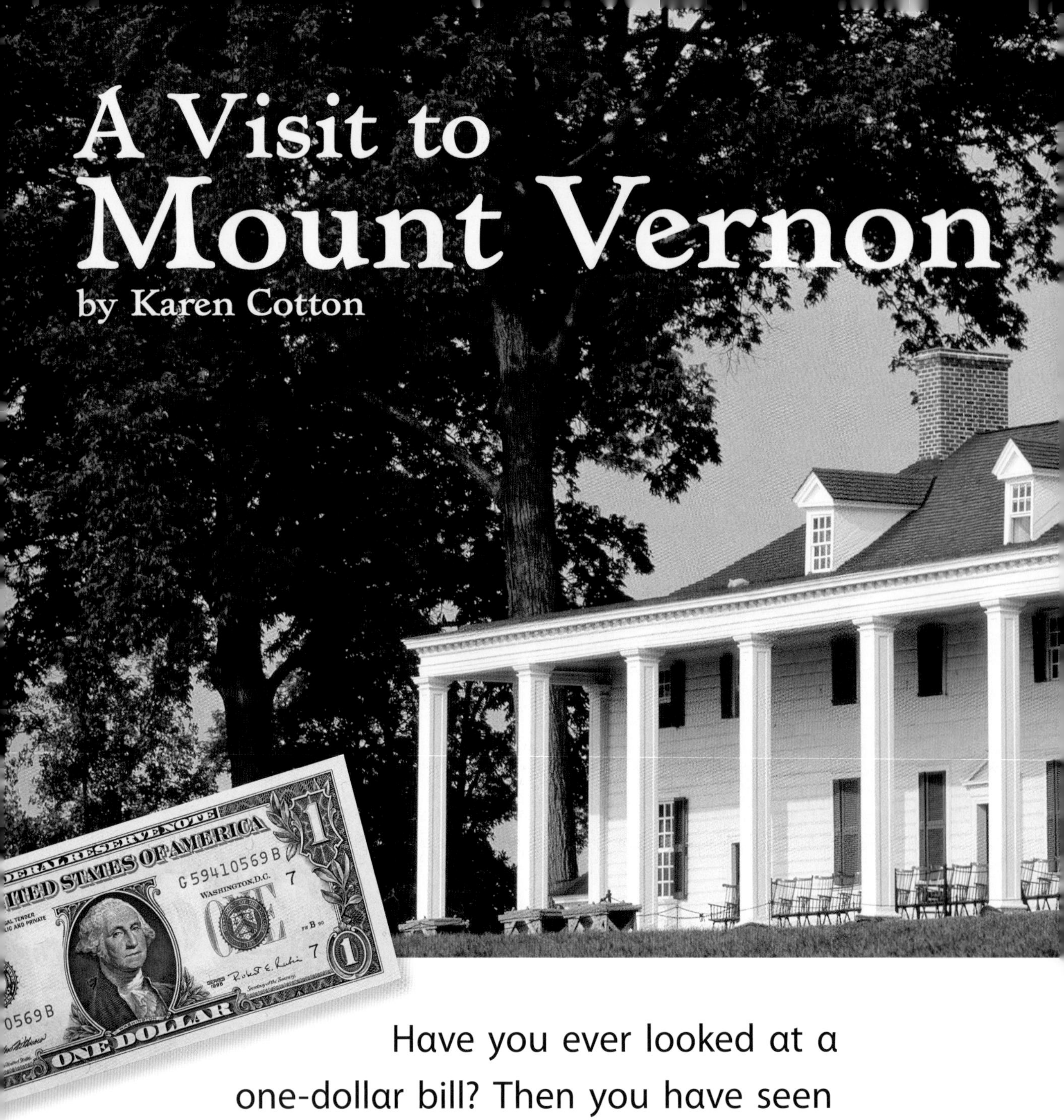

Have you ever looked at a one-dollar bill? Then you have seen a picture of George Washington. He lived in the 1700s. He helped make the new nation called the United States of America. Washington was also its first president.

Have you ever been to Mount Vernon? It is open all year now. It used to be George Washington's home. Mount Vernon includes the mansion, or big house, where Washington lived. It also includes a lot of land.

Mount Vernon has farmlands and gardens. Look at this flower garden. It is one of the gardens at Mount Vernon.

Washington left Mount Vernon at times, but he liked to return. He had a good life there. Washington was a farmer. He tried new ways of farming. He was the first person in the United States to own mules. He was sure that they were better than horses for farm work.

Today visitors come to Mount Vernon. They want to see how Washington lived. Visitors can go into the mansion. They can see Washington's bed.

Visitors can see some of Washington's clothes, too. These clothes were mainly made of linen, cotton, or wool.

Look at the buttons. They are made of shells and metals. Silver is one of the metals that was used. See the silver coffee pot?

Visitors can see Washington's razor, too. He shaved with it. Have you ever seen a razor like it?

In the old days, many visitors came to visit Washington at Mount Vernon. They often ate dinner with him. This photo shows the kitchen at Mount Vernon. In Washington's time, cooks used the fireplace for cooking. Look at all the utensils, such as spoons and forks. What is the floor made of?

Look at the pots, pans, platters, and dishes. These things are in a pantry, or storeroom, at Mount Vernon. Which of the objects look like things that people use today?

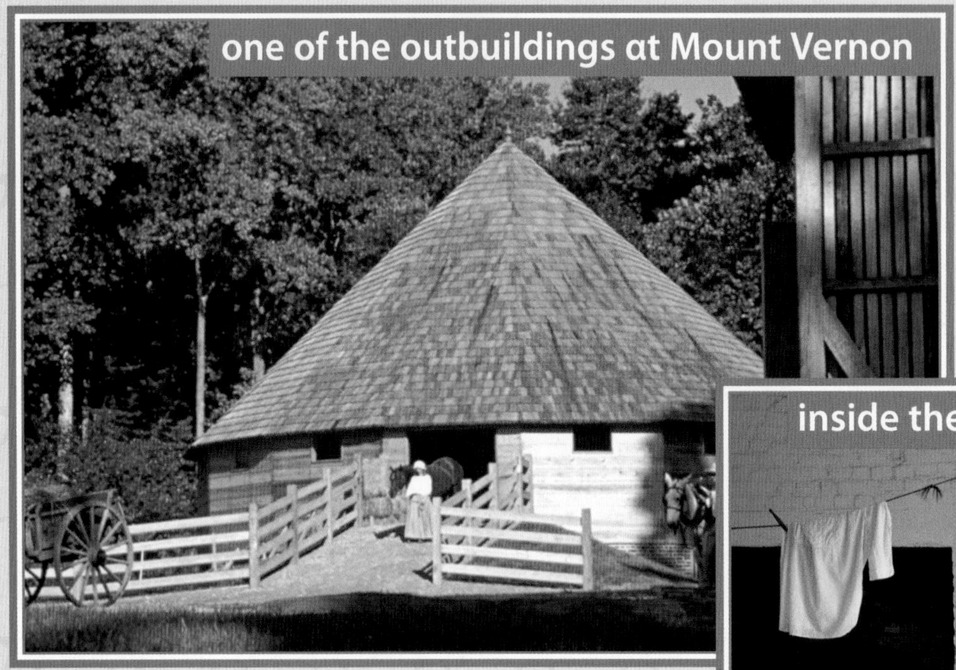
one of the outbuildings at Mount Vernon

inside the wash house

Mount Vernon also has many outbuildings. The wash house is one of them. Workers once did laundry in the wash house. They would launder clothes, towels, and linens. Do you see the clean laundry hanging up to dry?

The salthouse is another outbuilding. Long ago, fish was salted and stored in barrels. Fish was "cured" with salt to keep it from spoiling. The people at Mount Vernon ate a lot of salt-cured fish.

Bacon and hams were smoked and stored in the smokehouse. Smoke kept meats from rotting. Washington and his visitors could eat the smoked meats much, much later.

There are a number of things to see at Mount Vernon. Would you like to visit?

Words with Schwa

Read these words.

flower	razor	barrel	garden	pantry
towel	seen	kitchen	person	utensil

Find the words with schwa.
Use letters to build them.

g a r d e n

Talk Together

Choose words from the box above to tell your partner what you see in each place.

I see a towel in the kitchen.

Final Syllables with -ent, -ant

Look at each picture. Read the word.

Example:

pres**ent**

stud**ent**

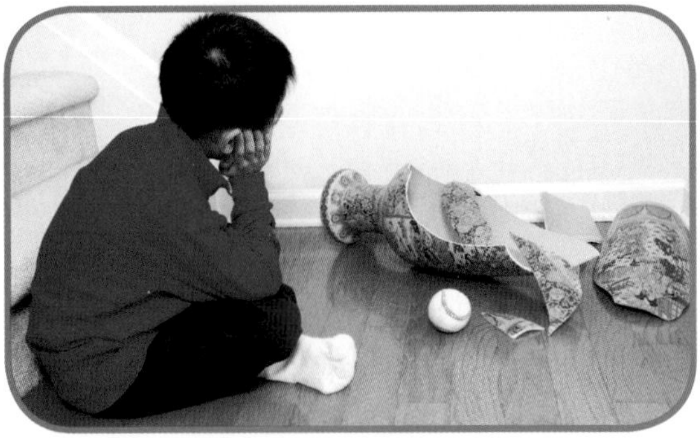

accid**ent**

hydr**ant**

High Frequency Words

- ate
- bed
- big
- came
- floor
- home
- left
- life
- new
- sure

Key Words

Look at the pictures. Read the sentences.

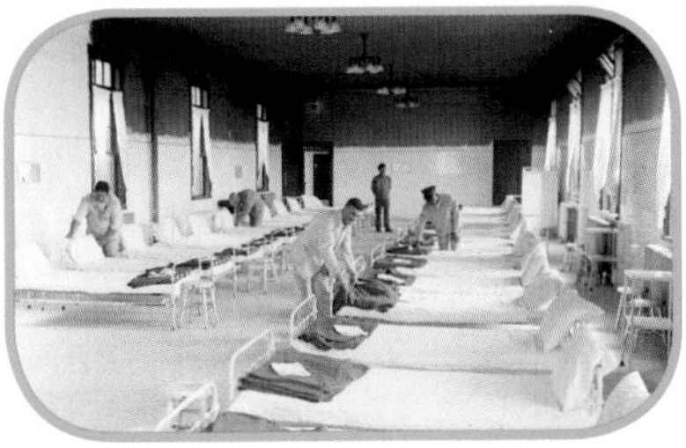

They Left Their Homes

1. Many immigrants **left home** and **came** to America.
2. They were **sure life** would be better.
3. They **ate** their meals at the **big** immigration station.
4. The **floor** was packed with people.
5. A sick person could rest in a **bed** there.
6. Soon they would leave to start a **new** life.

How do you think these immigrants felt?

Phonics Games

NGReach.com

Immigrants Stopped Here

by Luc Marchant

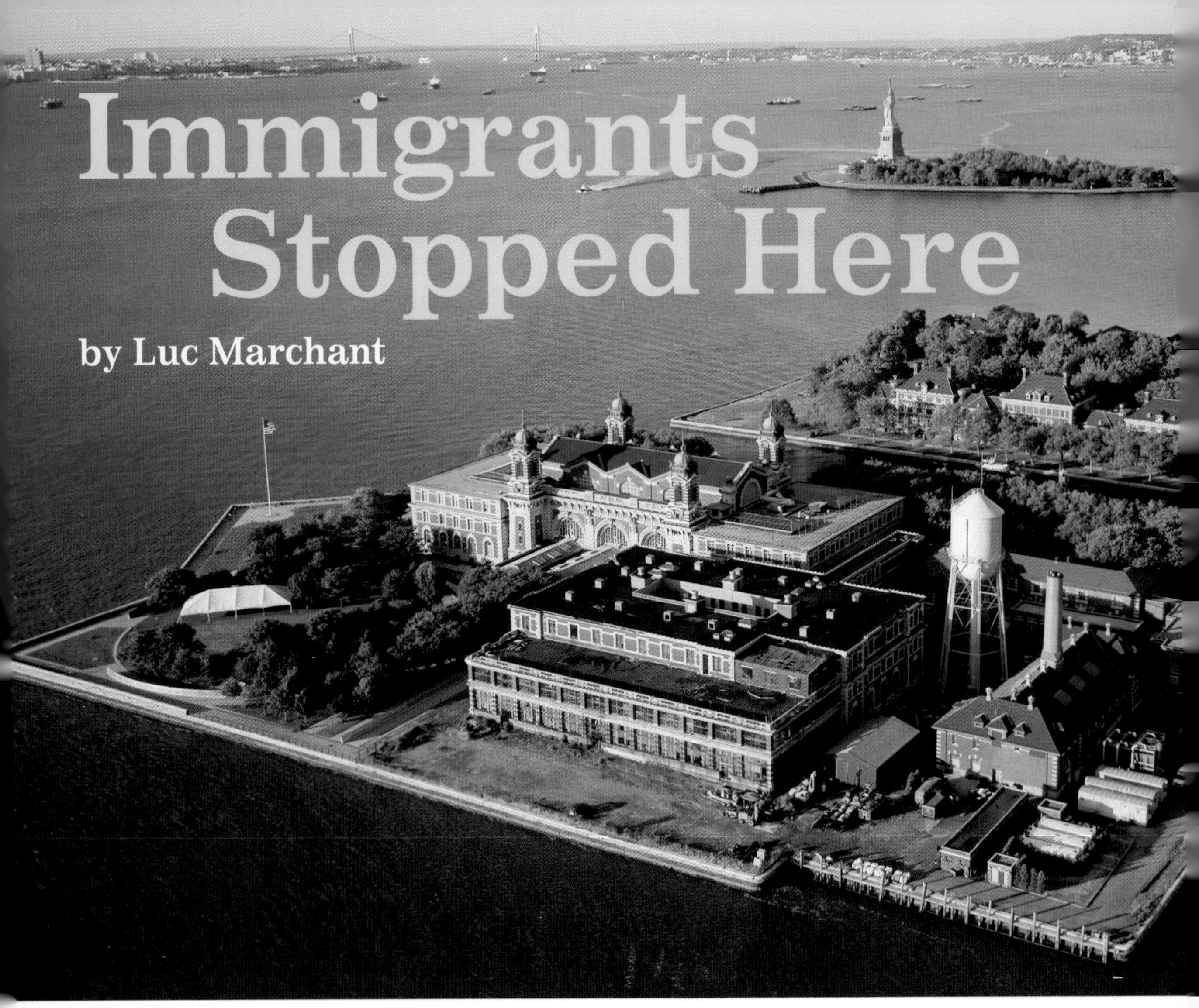

Ellis Island is in New York Harbor. It was an immigration station from 1892 to 1954. More than 12,000,000 immigrants came to the United States through Ellis Island. Immigrants came from many distant countries. They left their homes and boarded crowded ships to get here. They hoped for a new and better life.

Annie Moore was the first immigrant to pass through this immigration station. She came from Ireland. Annie was just 15. She and her two younger brothers came to join their parents. Today you can see this statue of Annie at Ellis Island.

Immigrants came from different backgrounds. Many were workers, farmers, or servants—like the two peasants from Poland in the photo. Look at those large bundles! A few were musicians and artists with a lot of talent. Which one is the musician?

Look at this Greek family. Can you see the big suitcase? Which parent is carrying the infant? You can tell the photo is old. How? Look at the garments. The clothing styles are quite different from today's styles.

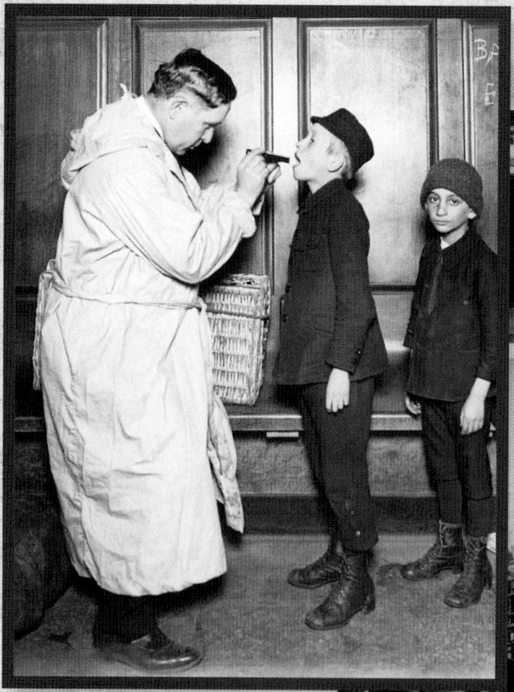

Each recent arrival got a health exam. Immigrants stood on the floor in the Great Hall. Inspectors looked at each arrival's papers, too. Healthy arrivals with papers in order could start their new lives in the United States.

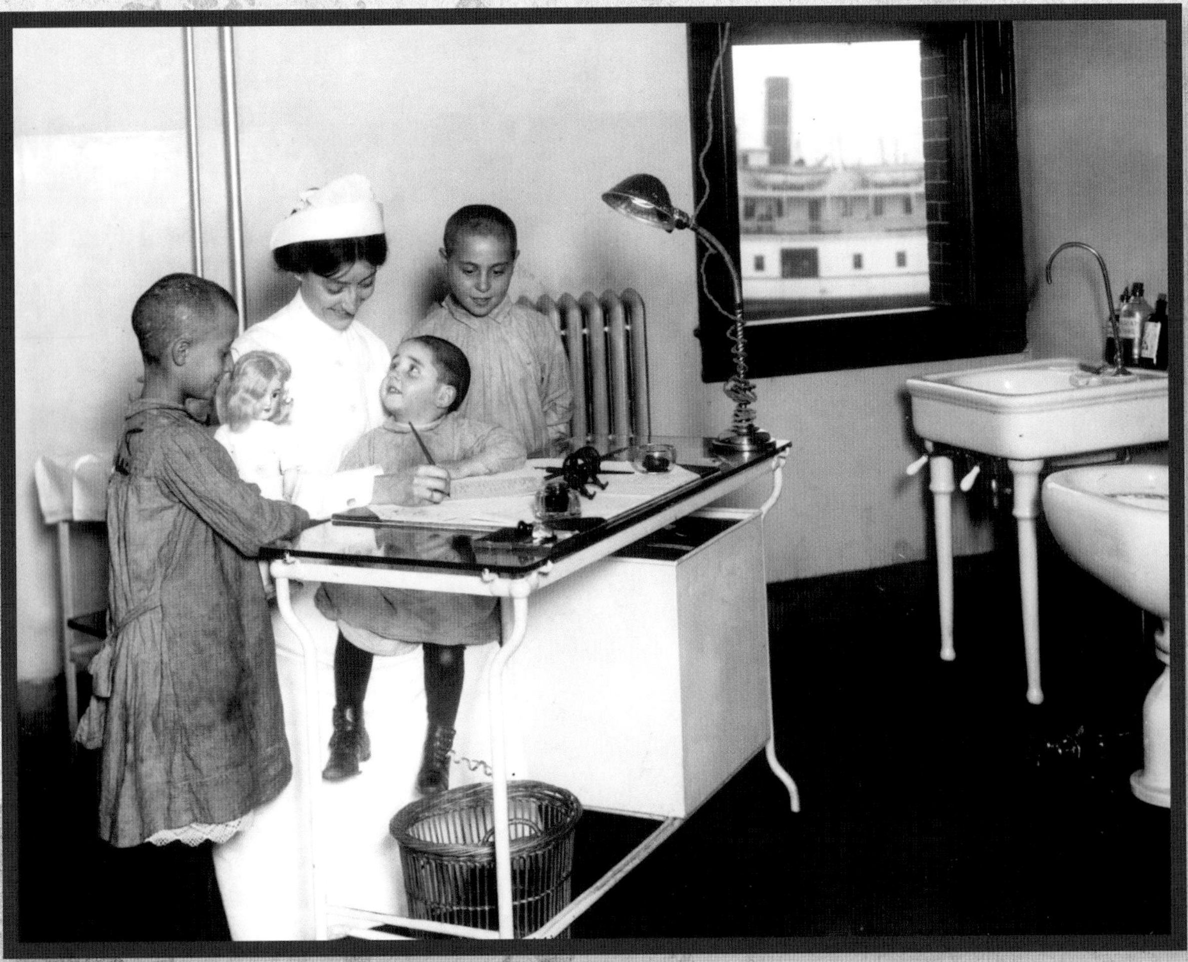

Sick arrivals had to stay on Ellis Island. They were sent to the hospital. It was important for them to get well. Then they could leave the immigration station.

The Angel Island Immigration Station opened in 1910. It stayed open for 30 years. About 1,000,000 immigrants came there. No one is sure of the exact number.

Two Immigration Stations

	Ellis Island	Angel Island
Location	NY, East Coast	CA, West Coast
Year Opened	1892	1910
Year Closed	1954	1940
Number of Immigrants Who Passed Through	More than 12,000,000	About 1,000,000

Look at the chart. How was Angel Island different from Ellis Island?

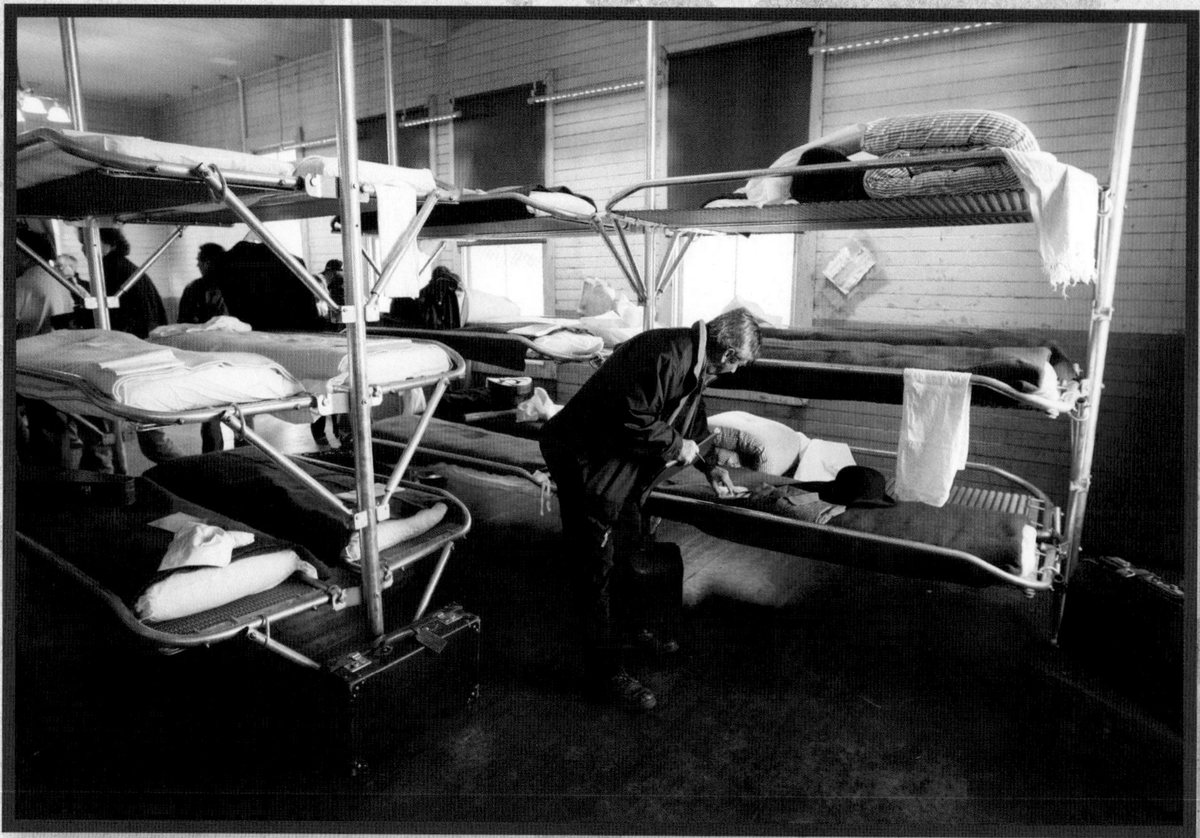

Immigrants at Angel Island got health exams, too. They answered questions. Many immigrants spent weeks at the immigration station. Some people stayed there longer. They ate meals there. They slept in beds like these.

poem from Angel Island

Most of the Angel Island immigrants were Chinese. While they waited and waited to leave, some put poems in Chinese on the walls. The smaller photo shows a copy of a real poem. In it, the writer tells that he feels like a bird in a cage.

Angel Island Immigration Station closed in 1940. Ellis Island closed in 1954. Both were turned into state parks. They were set up to help visitors learn about the immigrants who passed through these places.

Final Syllables with -ent, -ant

Read these words.

distant	recent	garment	suitcase	slept
infant	parent	important	husband	immigrant

Find the words with final **-ent** or **-ant** syllables.
Use letters to build them.

d i s t a n t

Talk Together

Choose words from the box above to ask your partner questions about each picture.

Do you see the immigrant holding the infant?

Help Isabel Pack

Help Isabel find the things she needs to pack. Look at the picture with a partner. Take turns reading the items and pointing to answers. Find these things:

1. a new garment with a silver button
2. a towel left on the bed of her home
3. a big wrapped present on the floor
4. a picture of Isabel's parents with an infant
5. a dinner platter (She has to wash it. It still has some of the food she ate for supper!)

Acknowledgments
Grateful acknowledgment is given to the authors, artists, photographers, museums, publishers, and agents for permission to reprint copyrighted material. Every effort has been made to secure the appropriate permission. If any omissions have been made or if corrections are required, please contact the Publisher.

Photographic Credits
CVR Jim Pickerell/Stock Connection Blue/Alamy Images. **2** (bl) Sandra van der Steen/Shutterstock. (br) PhotoDisc/Getty Images. (cl) ArnoldW/Shutterstock. (cr) Oleg Seleznev/iStockphoto. (tl) Iconotec. (tr) Artville. **3** (br) Liz Garza Williams/Hampton-Brown/National Geographic School Publishing. (cl) The Granger Collection, New York. (cr) Joe Raedle/Getty Images. (tr) Carolyn M Carpenter/Shutterstock. **4** (cl) Artville. **4-5** Walter Bibikow/JAI/Corbis. **6** Peter Finger/Corbis. **7** (cr) Dan Dry/National Geographic Image Collection. (tl) The Granger Collection, New York. **8** (r) Gavin Ashworth/Courtesy of the Mount Vernon Ladies' Association. (tl) By courtesy of Mount Vernon Ladies Association./Richard Bryant/Arcaid/Alamy Images. **9** (c) Mark Finkenstaedt/Courtesy of the Mount Vernon Ladies' Association. (tl) Gavin Ashworth/Courtesy of the Mount Vernon Ladies' Association. (tr) Gavin Ashworth/Courtesy of the Mount Vernon Ladies' Association. **10** Photo Network Stock/Grant Heilman Photography. **11** Ted Spiegel/Corbis. **12** (cr) Richard Bryant/ Publication by courtesy of Mount Vernon Ladies Association./Arcaid. (t) Courtesy of the Mount Vernon Ladies' Association. **13** (cr) Ekaterina Starshaya/Shutterstock. (t) Courtesy of the Mount Vernon Ladies' Association. **14** Courtesy of the Mount Vernon Ladies' Association. **15** (bc) David Dixon/Garden Picture Library/Photolibrary. (bl) Simone van den Berg/Shutterstock. (cr) Liz Garza Williams/Hampton-Brown/National Geographic School Publishing. **16** (bl) fotosav/Shutterstock. (br) Thomas M Perkins/Shutterstock. (cl) Pierre Yu/Shutterstock. (tl) Ivonne Wierink/Shutterstock. (tr) Monkey Business Images/Shutterstock. **17** (b) Liz Garza Williams/Hampton-Brown/National Geographic School Publishing. (cl) Corbis. (tl) Augustus F. Sherman/National Geographic Image Collection. (tr) Bettmann/Corbis. **18-19** Michael S. Yamashita/National Geographic Image Collection. **19** (bg) Peter Zelei/iStockphoto. (t) Sculptor Jeanne Rynhart/Photographer Mike Booth/Alamy Images. **20** (bg) Peter Zelei/iStockphoto. (cr) The Granger Collection, New York. (tl) Bettmann/Corbis. **21** Bettmann/Corbis. **22** (tl) Bettmann/Corbis. (tr) The Granger Collection, New York. **22-23** (bg) Peter Zelei/iStockphoto. **23** (t) Culver Pictures/The Art Archive. **24** (t) Time Life Pictures/National Archives/Getty Images. **24-25** (bg) Peter Zelei/iStockphoto. **26** (bg) Peter Zelei/iStockphoto. (t) Justin Sullivan/Getty Images. **27** (inset) Philip Gould/Corbis. (t) The Granger Collection, New York. **28** (bg) Peter Zelei/iStockphoto. (c) Pjard/Shutterstock. (tl) Justin Sullivan/ Getty Images. **29** (bl) Lewis W Hine/Hulton Archive/Getty Images. (br) Ernst Haas/Getty Images. (cr) Liz Garza Williams/Hampton-Brown/National Geographic School Publishing.

Illustrator Credits
30-31 Peter Grosshauer

National Geographic School Publishing
Hampton-Brown
www.NGSP.com

Printed in the USA.
Quad Graphics, Leominster, MA

ISBN:978-0-7362-8086-0

17 18 19
10 9 8 7 6